THE
JOURNEY

*The Uncharted Adventure
Toward Your Dream*

DEBORAH STRICKLIN

The Journey

by Deborah Rae Stricklin

Cover design by Martijn van Tilborgh

Published by Dream Releaser Publishing

Print ISBN: 978-1-943294-13-8
eBook ISBN: 978-1-943294-14-5

The Journey is also available on Amazon Kindle, Barnes & Noble Nook and Apple iBooks.

Contents

FOREWORD 5

INTRODUCTION 9

THE DREAM...11

REDEFINING SUCCESS..15

EMBRACING PREPARATION 23

TENDING THE HEART...31

KEEPING AN OPEN HAND..41

GAINING INFLUENCE...49

LEARNING TO WAIT 57

REFUSING TO QUIT...65

Foreword

SOME TIME AGO, I asked my firstborn daughter, Kirsten, to write about dreaming, legacy, and preparation, thinking I would use some of her thoughts in The Journey. I began to sense that what she was about to give me would end up as the foreword to this book. As I read what she wrote, I struggled with the focus. I want God to always remain the center, not anything I've done. However, her words are powerful regarding legacy. So, as you read the following, focus on the faithfulness of a God who allows us to participate in passing His blessing from one generation to the next.

Kirsten writes:

Many parents want to prepare their children for life by providing them with *things*—financial stability, a top-notch education, and a good work ethic. It seems that a slightly smaller percentage of parents want to provide their children with the *keys* to a successful life, such as a value for honesty, integrity, common sense, and respect. There is still a smaller handful of parents, though, who go one step farther in their provision to their children. They grasp the concept of *legacy*—truly shaping and guiding their children's lives for the future by living an extraordinary life in front of them. That's my mom.

Merriam-Webster's Dictionary defines *legacy* as "something that happened in the past or that comes from someone in the past." So, legacy can be a fiscal gift; it can be that antique ring that has been in the family for four generations; it can be a last name that "lives on" through a family's sons; but it can also be something more. Legacy can be a life well-lived that children, grandchildren, and great-grandchildren can learn from and apply to their own lives. It can include choices, decisions, and the influence of a single person who chooses to live differently—and daringly.

My mom is leaving for me a legacy. I look around and see people who are content with their day jobs, their busy schedules, and their "I-go-to-church-on-Sundays" Christian lives. I look at my mom, and I see someone different. I see a person who has laid down her life to pursue Christ. She has resisted the social norm, daring to do what seems illogical in order to know the presence of God. As a result, God has placed in her heart a dream bigger than she can describe, and yet she holds on to it with everything in her. My mom doesn't give up this dream in adversity, in pain, or in misunderstanding. She holds steady, trusting the Lord to bring her dream to pass. Through this, she has shown me how to dream.

Dreaming isn't an easy thing. Movies, books, and inspiring speeches encourage us to "dream big" and "dare to dream," but it's not that simple. I have had the privilege of walking beside my mom through the mud and sludge involved in waiting patiently for a dream. She has slogged through years of financial stress, marital struggles, and attacks from people she thought cared most for her. And, even still, as she waits before the Lord for her dream, she is not bitter. She is not judgmental. She is, in fact, more loving and filled with joy than she's ever been because of the presence of God. She has modeled before me the true meaning of James 1:2-4 (NKJV): "My brethren, count it all joy when you fall into various trials, knowing that the testing of your faith produces patience. But let patience have its perfect work, that you may be perfect and complete, lacking nothing." She has taught me how to wait.

If I'm honest, patience is one of my least favorite virtues. It takes away my ability to be proactive and puts the control in another person's hands. Think about it—every time you have to be patient, isn't it because someone caused a traffic jam that someone else has to clean up, someone hasn't checked their calendar and given you an answer, or someone is chatting about the weather with the bank teller while you're standing behind them tapping your toe? Being patient before God puts the control in *His* hands rather than in our own. It's a tough thing to do! By watching my mother do this—not easily, but through intense prayer and fighting the desire to act outside of God's timing—I have seen the benefits of patience.

Being a bystander of someone waiting patiently is at times agonizing. I often found myself asking God, "Why?" on her behalf. Through this period of waiting, though, my mom has been sharing with me what she has learned from God and the Bible. She has chosen to view it as a time of preparation rather than a time of torturous patience, and that has expanded my perspective more than I can explain. As I'm walking through my own (smaller!) trial of waiting, I look to her example of how to seek God in preparation for the next step in my life. She has modeled preparation for me.

I'm almost 23 years old, and I have no idea what my future holds. I don't know who I'll marry, what career I'll have, or what my family will look like. I have no clue what joys and what pains and what difficult times my life will hold. I do know, though, that I have a legacy to look to. I have a mom who has exhibited for me a life of passionate devotion to the things of God. She has lived in front of me how to respond to all situations—good and bad—with a Christ-like attitude. I'm not saying she's perfect—no one is; I'm saying that her decision to strive after God with everything in her has spoken to me more than her words ever could. So, thank you, Mom—you've left a legacy that has already changed my life.

Strength and honor are her clothing;
She shall rejoice in time to come.
She opens her mouth with wisdom,
And on her tongue is the law of kindness.
She watches over the ways of her household,
And does not eat the bread of idleness.
Her children rise up and call her blessed;
Her husband also, and he praises her:
"Many daughters have done well,
But you excel them all."
Charm is deceitful and beauty is passing,
But a woman who fears the Lord, she shall be praised.

— Proverbs 31:25-30 (NKJV)

I love you, Mom!

— Kirsten

Introduction

I'VE ALWAYS KNOWN I'd write a book. I just didn't think it would be now. Most people who author books write from their success, remembering the path they walked to arrive at the apex of their purpose. It seems awkward to write in the middle of the journey, but perhaps that's what's needed—a voice of encouragement in the midst of the process.

Ah, the *almighty process*—we either learn to love it and embrace it or to remain in constant friction with it. I've always been one who simply wanted to arrive wherever I was going, not endure the journey getting there. Although teleportation seemed the answer to my angst in life, God certainly had a different plan in mind. Rather than catering to my turbo boost existence, in His sovereign wisdom, He chose to slow me down and teach me to enjoy the journey. I would have never believed this was possible—to enjoy the journey (or to slow me down!). What appeared to me to be the nuisance of time wasted in "getting there" turned out to be the very fuel for my transformation. It is for you as well.

My goal in writing the chapters that follow is first and foremost to provide encouragement that you probably need if you're in the middle of a long journey of preparation. *Hope with me as we walk toward God's intended purpose for our lives.* Because I know He's for me, not against me, I'm confident I'll arrive smack dab in the center of His will, as you can, too. I've told my children (as a statement of faith) for years, "I'm on a collision course with my destiny." If you are struggling with those words in the midst of *your* process, keep reading. You'll be shouting that phrase by the time we're finished! God will complete what He has started, and He is never late.

> ...these things I plan won't happen right away. Slowly, steadily, surely, the time approaches when the vision will be fulfilled. If it seems slow, wait patiently, for it will surely take place. It will not be delayed. — Habakkuk 2:3 (NLT)

Thank you for allowing me to share my journey with you. We'll examine the answers to the most important question each of us can ask: *What am I learning in the process?*

The Dream

GOD IS AS UNIQUE in delivering dreams as He is in Creation itself. For many people, God gives a clear, panoramic picture of their life's vision and then methodically brings it to pass, almost like checking off the items on a list. For others (such as me), God offers just enough information along the way to keep us moving in the right direction, but the end goal only comes into focus as we round the last corner toward the finish line. Perhaps God knew that I would rush headlong for the finish line if He gave me the vision all at once. Maybe He knew it would seem so far out of reach that I would shrink back prematurely. Whatever His reason, He has drawn me along through the fog on the journey toward my purpose. Has it been difficult? I will answer with a resounding, "YES!" But the faith and trust in Him that has been etched into my spirit as a result of His methods in my life has been worth the difficulty.

My parents chose to name me Deborah. Their choice wasn't because they just liked the way it sounded or because it was a popular baby name. The Biblical judge and leader of the Israelite nation, Deborah, was their deliberate role model for me. I grew up in church, gave my heart to Jesus at an early age, and faithfully walked with God. At about ten years old, I had a significant onslaught of fear and doubt in my salvation. My mother was wise enough to ask our pastor at that time to kneel with me at the altar and pray over my life. When he finished praying, my fear subsided, and my doubt never returned. Not long after that episode, my mother had a dream regarding the influence that God would bring through my life. She dreamed of a large, solid oak tree with branches that spread wide in every direction. Nestled within its branches was wildlife of every kind, safe from the attack of predators. Under its branches, families ate and played together, sheltered from the heat of the day. They enjoyed peace, joy, and nourishment. Her dream was the sort that imprints on the mind, never to be forgotten. As I got older, she relayed the dream to me, leaving it with me to ponder in my heart.

As a young mother, deep in worship one Sunday night at Cornerstone Church, God showed me a triangle with these three items, one at each vertex: education, public speaking, and healing. He explained that these would be the three components He would intertwine to create my future. So, it was with that small amount of information that I began my quest to fulfill my destiny. As a career educator, my unquenchable desire to learn compelled me to obtain my master's degree in education, and then later, the completion of my ministerial ordination courses.

Now, as I look back over the last few years, I can see that the education portion of the triangle could also be named discipleship. As I have poured my knowledge and experience into the children and adults around me, I have reveled in watching their growth.

The draw to begin speaking in front of people fought against my quiet nature. I took each opportunity given to me to practice the art of public speaking. I would carefully plan my words, my time, and the effect I wanted to leave on my audience. Again, during worship one Sunday, God drew me to my knees and asked, "Will you preach My gospel?" I told Him that although I had no idea how He would accomplish that through me, my answer was yes. Eventually, through much practice teaching Sunday school and topical classes, I learned to allow the Holy Spirit to flow through my speaking, finally bringing me to enjoyment delivering God's messages.

Healing is the third part of the triangle. I love praying for people, specifically for healing. As I have spent time praying with people at the altars and in hospitals, I have come to realize that this is a vital part of what God has in mind for the days yet to come. I am very sure I have only seen the tip of the iceberg with each aspect of this triangular vision, but that moment with God during worship started me on the course that will eventually lead to the fulfillment of my purpose. I look forward to serving God's people in discipleship, preaching, and healing. Although the waiting seems long, I am incredibly excited about all that God is yet to do.

The following illustration from John Ortberg's book, *If You Want to Walk on Water, You've Got to Get Out of the Boat*, is one I used in a Sunday school lesson I taught some time ago titled *Learning to Wait Well*. The story so beautifully illustrates waiting on God's incredible timing.

"What does it look like to wait with patient trust? Henri Nouwen gave us a picture of patient trust not long before he died in 1996. Writing about some trapeze artists who became good friends of his, he explained that there is a very special relationship between the flyer and the catcher... As the flyer is swinging high above the crowd, the moment comes when he lets go of the trapeze, when he arcs out into the air. For that moment, which must feel like an eternity, the flyer is suspended in nothingness. It is too late to reach back for the trapeze. There is no going back now. However, it is too soon to be grasped by the one who will catch him. He cannot accelerate the catch. In that moment, his job is to be as still and motionless as he can. 'The flyer must never try to catch the catcher,' the trapeze artist told Nouwen. 'He must wait in absolute trust. The catcher will catch him. But he must wait. His job is not to flail about in anxiety. In fact, if he does, it could kill him. His job is to be still. To wait. And to wait is the hardest work of all.'"

Growing up as a competitive gymnast, probably the thing I miss most about those years of gymnastics is the feeling of unsuspended flight (every once in a while, I still go find a trampoline to jump on!). As I allow God to lead me through the maze of patient trust in the fulfillment of the dream, there's a return to that feeling of unsuspended flight (this time spiritually instead of physically). And, I'm finding that joy and freedom are close companions to trust—*trust in the One who will surely catch me.*

Chapter 1

Redefining Success

"Many of life's failures are people who did not realize how close they were to success when they gave up." — Thomas A. Edison

I T'S EASY TO DEFINE success as the title conferred upon someone after going through the paces of reaching a goal. Once success is achieved, all of the hard work in getting there seems a distant memory, hardly worth honorable mention. But depending on the depth of difficulty, years invested, and sacrifices made, the "getting there" is truly worth the focus of our attention.

When we understand that our success is the product of the journey, we begin to see "getting there" in a different light. The journey is actually what defines us, what forms us. *Success is simply a by-product of the person we've become during the journey.*

As I look back over the last few years, I recall what I would identify as critical influences that have shaped me. There have been a handful of key people who have served as mentors in my life. Their influence was brief, yet powerful. I've found myself complaining to God on more than one occasion that He has never allowed any one person to remain as a mentor to me for more than a brief period. It's as if I would lean too heavily on a person if He allowed it. God wants my rapt attention, but has graciously given me moments of comfort and direction that mentoring relationships can bring.

Because God's purpose for my life is pastoral in nature, most of my mentors have been associate pastors who have served on staff at Cornerstone Nashville. Over the last eighteen years, each of these people has brought a different aspect of encouragement at just the right moment. Proverbs 25:11 (NLT) reminds us that "timely advice is as lovely as golden apples in a silver basket." In the early years of my dream development, Pastor Glenda cautioned me to give my heart time to grow into my calling when everything in me wanted to launch. Pastor Bob reaffirmed God's hand on my life during my darkest days when my dream appeared dead. Pastor Danny allowed me to serve alongside him while my heart needed time to heal. Pastor Greg consistently gave me ministry opportunities to grow when I felt invisible. Pastor Dave spoke the wise words, "Debbie, <u>let God bring it to you</u>," when my desperation to see the dream fulfilled nearly caused me to charge headlong in the wrong direction. And, the common thread running through these eighteen years of preparation has come from Pastor Maury Davis; he has simply taught me to keep dreaming and never, never give up. My gratitude for each of these people is forever extended toward them.

I must also mention that although these mentors have given me needed encouragement along the way, my closest companion has been the Holy Spirit. When I feel alone, He is my friend. When I doubt, He is my confidence. When I need guidance, He is my wisdom. I have learned to lean into His leading and sweet presence. With a gentle voice, He speaks. Learning to live with a quiet spirit allows me to hear Him clearly. It takes deliberate practice to produce a quiet spirit. Once the dialogue opens though, you'll have no desire to return to a distracted existence.

Another significant influence is that my world is flooded with books—books that cause me to dream, books that shift my perspective, and books that drive me to my knees in prayer. I remember in my early twenties going through what some might call a spiritual desert or "dark night of the soul," a term Richard Foster uses in his writing. It was Foster's book *Celebration of Discipline* that jolted me out of my sinking depression. Among the hundreds of titles I have voraciously consumed over the years, a few stand out as pivotal along my journey.

Visioneering by Andy Stanley was one of the first books I read about learning to dream. It inspired me to believe that the seeds God had planted in my heart truly could be the beginnings of my destiny. I still smile every time my eyes drift over its title on my bookshelf. John Ortberg's book, *If You Want to Walk on Water, You've Got to Get Out of the Boat*, encouraged me to risk personal comfort to move toward my dream. I have referenced his material in countless talks I've delivered over the years.

17

People who spend a great portion of their time reading usually have one book that they return to over and over again. That book for me is _Run with the Horses_ by Eugene Peterson. Peterson's examination of the life of Jeremiah the prophet connected with me in a way no other book has. I found in Jeremiah a similar heartbeat, a relentless pursuit of obedience and excellence toward God. Jeremiah's life often met with difficult circumstances, but his commitment to fulfill God's purpose remained paramount. I return to _Run with the Horses_ each year to re-identify with Jeremiah's calling and strength.

Reading is imperative. Stretching the boundaries of human existence can't take place if we only experience the daily grind. Dr. William Inge writes, "If we spend sixteen hours a day dealing with tangible things and only five minutes a day dealing with God, is it any wonder that tangible things are two hundred times more real to us than God?" The opposite is true as well. Meditating on _Him_ causes us to see into _His_ realm, making _His_ desires, _His_ dreams, and _His_ plans so real to us that we find ourselves living in two worlds—the visible and the invisible. _Bringing into the visible that which is invisible, then, becomes our great adventure._ So, no matter the busyness of life, make time to read what inspires and ignites your passions. You'll discover that certain authors connect with your way of thinking. Stay current with their recent publications as you move on to other authors as well.

Worship music is also a major source of inspiration to the passionate heart. It can quiet a restless spirit and allow us to move our emotions from fear to faith.

We need the repetition of Scripture, and worship music can provide those reminders of God's Word. In one popular praise chorus, the phrase "You make all things work together for my good" is repeated frequently and becomes etched into our thought process. It reminds us that God is constantly using every situation in our lives to enhance the outcome, the "who" that He created us to be. He will truly work all things together for our good as we stay submitted to His purpose and direction in our lives. In recent years, I've added hymns back into my music choices. Many of them have been given a contemporary twist, making their beauty come alive once more. Music has always been an influential part of history, and it can create for us today, as well, an atmosphere of peace and faith.

Circumstances (both victorious and challenging) are also an ever-present source of influence. I'm glad He's so good at using the hurtful situations of our lives, as well as the good. They, too, shape us during the journey. It's those hurtful moments in life that I want to focus on for the next few pages.

We want to believe that the journey to our dreams will be filled only with people who encourage and inspire us. Let me share a little secret with you—the bigger your dream, the fewer people you'll have standing beside you at some of the most critical moments along the journey. And, sometimes, those who oppose you most are closest to you. Those you relied on in the past might suddenly scatter. The bigger you dream, the further you must stretch. Not everyone wants to stretch. Not everyone will travel the journey with you. Those are difficult words. Like toddlers, people can be incredibly resistant to change. They like their world in the nice, neat packages they've created. Dreams require risk, which doesn't come in nice, neat packages. Risk is messy. Risk is scary. Risk is unpredictable and unmanageable. A risky step of faith will often cause the insecure family member or friend to lash out in unexpected ways.

When God delivers a dream to the human heart, it's delivered to the individual. One of the most costly mistakes dreamers make is believing that the people around them are as invested and passionate about the dream as they are. Nothing could be further from the truth. That's why risky steps of faith can be threatening to those around us. Prepare, as best you can, those people closest to you who will be affected by your decisions.

Marriage ushers in another consideration in pursuing your dream. Because man and woman become one flesh under the covenant of marriage, you must seek God's direction for your life as a couple. Pray together, and be in unity. Perhaps a season of prayer is needed before you can approach your spouse about a dream God has laid on your heart. Rather than springing it on your spouse immediately, spend the needed time praying for open hearts and unity. The main objective is to remain in an attitude of prayer and submission before the Lord.

You'll also find support in some of the unlikeliest places. God has a way of positioning someone at just the right moment to be your advocate. Don't look for a team of cheerleaders to surround you. Encouragement usually comes in one strategically placed person at a time who will keep you moving forward.

We all desire nurturing companionship, and in terms of bringing forth a dream, God is the ultimate companion. It's easy in the busyness of life to want to *accomplish* rather than take time to *connect* with the God who created you. But God isn't interested in what you can accomplish outside of relationship with Him. It's the relationship itself that He desires. It's you that He wants. Prayer and meditation are often harder work than meeting deadlines and reaching goals. When we meet with God, we have to open our hearts to His presence, which is not a welcome activity for many. And, yet, that's the very place He wants us.

It's through that time in His presence that your true transformation will take place. One of my most frequently prayed prayers is, "God, shine Your light in the hidden corners of my heart. Bring to light those areas of my heart that need Your touch." Luke 11:36 (NLT) tells us, "If you are filled with light, with no dark corners, then your whole life will be radiant, as though a floodlight is shining on you." Having an open, accessible heart toward God is your lifeline. His ability to guide you, discipline you, and bless you lies in the proper position of your heart.

The Word of God (the Bible) is an irreplaceable component of influence. Without it, God has little access to our thought process. The Word will transform our thinking if we'll open it, read it, hear it preached, and meditate on it. Too many Christians today let their church service be the main dish and their own Bible reading the occasional dessert. The opposite should take place. We must hunger after God, pursuing Him because our lives and our purpose depend on it. Pray that God would open your eyes as you read His Word. He is eager to share beautiful hidden treasures reserved for those who seek Him.

God's definition of success is a life that has been yielded to His use. That is not an overnight achievement! Andy Stanley wisely writes, "Rare is the visionary who is able to maintain a spirit of dependency and humility in the face of public success. So God works overtime to ground, strengthen, stretch, and mature our faith in the initial stages of the visioneering process. Our ability to go the distance depends on it... God uses the time before our vision is launched to fasten our faith to Him. He allows us to rev our engines in the starting blocks long enough for us to overheat and shut down. He allows us to wait until our faith is in Him and Him alone. For that is our only hope for seeing our vision through to a truly successful ending." Settle into the *process* of becoming. He'll produce in you the solid foundation needed to carry out His dream for your life.

Chapter 2

Embracing Preparation

*"I will prepare, and some day my chance will come." —
Abraham Lincoln*

PREPARATION IS INTENSELY personal because our purpose is intensely personal. To the degree that we allow, God molds us to fit our purpose perfectly. The phrase "to the degree" represents the self-discipline, submission, persistence, hard work, and selflessness that it takes to let God have His way in us.

Preparation is, indeed, God's primary work in us. As He molds us to our purpose, He breaks down pride and fear, the two most formidable foes to achieving our destiny. Recently, I went running with my oldest daughter, Kirsten, through an older neighborhood, which included a cemetery. As we ran along the paved

23

lane among the gravestones, I began to wonder about the individuals buried there. Did they know God? Even if they knew Him, did they achieve their God-given purpose? Or, did they instead take their destiny with them to their grave? Are unearned millions, unwritten books, unpreached sermons, and unreached people groups lying in those marked graves? The sad truth is that Christians arrive in heaven every day never having fulfilled the purpose for which God created them.

It would be so much easier if God would just write our purpose for us on our birth certificates and then pave the way for achievement! Because His end goal is always to move us toward becoming more like Jesus Christ, He uses the journey to our destiny to shape us into the image of His Son. Once again, the journey becomes indispensable because the achievement of our destiny is simply the end result of "getting there."

Let's examine those two formidable foes I mentioned earlier—pride and fear. For those of us who are goal-oriented, task-driven people, pride is difficult to keep in check. Our sense of accomplishment is closely linked to self-reliance. We begin to believe that our accomplishments are based in our own strength, and pride easily rises. If not properly dealt with, pride can quickly lead to self-destruction and dream-destruction! One of the most effective combatants against pride is time in God's presence. As we spend time with Him, His greatness overshadows our sense of pride, and humility is birthed within our spirits.

Pride is so potentially damaging that God will employ various methods to redirect us toward dependence on Him. God often uses delays to interrupt the connection between our activity and our achievement, reminding us that He remains in control even when we think control belongs to us. Setbacks also have a way of knocking us off our self-made thrones. When life doesn't go as planned, we find ourselves heading back to the drawing board, which is usually where we last relied on Him.

God has used the last three years in my life to free me from pride's clutches. I would have thought that was best achieved through some humiliating experience (and, yes, I've had my share of those), but God's most effective method has been to bring me into His presence. Before I resigned my teaching position at school, I would rise at four in the morning, spend wonderful time in prayer and Bible study, go to work, grade papers during any unfilled moments, arrive home in time to go running, shower, throw together something for dinner, attend a ministry function, and fall into bed. I was proud of all I could fit into a day, and as if it was icing on my cupcake, I did it all well. Ministry was growing in my life, and I was working hard to be poised to walk into a full-time position when God opened the door. Without realizing it, though, I was feeding the kingdom of Debbie, not advancing the Kingdom of God. My diligent productivity was propelling me toward disaster. I'm so grateful God halted my rise to power. He used heartbreaking circumstances in my marriage and joblessness to slow me down.

Changing habits and well-worn paths is a process. It has taken three years of focused attention on Him to change my lifestyle rhythms and recreate this goal-driven person as a child of peace. God *is* peace. He *alone* is peace. Peace can't be found anywhere else—not in "relaxing" in front of the television, not in "hanging out" with friends, not in attending every ministry activity offered, and not in "playing" on the golf course or vacations. All of those activities are useful, but they don't produce peace. Our society has defined rest as any time spent away from the daily grind, but real rest and peace (mind, spirit, and body) come from being in the presence of God Himself.

It took me quite a while after resigning my job to stop feeling guilty for not having a full day. I felt the disapproval (real or imagined) from those nearest me for any unfilled time. I began busying my day with volunteer ministry activities. "Church needs" became my new employment. Serving in any way I was asked satisfied my busyness void. I was pleased to identify myself as "volunteer staff." Serving is good, right? Honestly, I loved it. I loved every minute of it. But, that was the problem. I was still loving the full schedule and the sense of achievement more than God Himself. Through a series of misunderstandings and a few very vocal, jealous church folks, I was side-lined from ministry. It turns out they had determined I must have manipulative, ulterior motives for the giving of my time. Church folks aren't always nice (in case you haven't figured that out). Yes, injustice happens. Yes, it's unfair. Yes, I was devastated. But, God was at work in me, and He truly does work *all* things together for our good. I had nowhere else to turn except His presence.

By this time, through my previous circumstances, I had learned to hide myself in Him. So, this time-out simply meant I had more time to be quiet, write, dwell in His presence, read His Word, and spend quality time building the relationships around me. I even had the privilege of participating in a city-wide ministry to feed the homeless people of Nashville one evening each week, which became such a joy to me in my place of solitude. Remember that God directs your steps, and He knows right where you are, even if it's not exactly where you want to be. So I told myself, if Old Testament Joseph could humbly endure betrayal, slavery, and prison, I could certainly let God have His way in me. And without exception, in His presence, humility rises, and pride falls.

While pride can drive us toward disaster, fear has a tendency to paralyze us. My daughter, Kirsten, and I recently completed our first triathlon. Training for the triathlon took months. We were already runners so we added swimming and biking. Neither one proved to be difficult until we moved from pool-swimming to open-water swimming. In the pool, there are few variables. Lap lanes serve as a guide, the water is clear, the temperature remains constant, and the distance is clearly marked. Not so in open-water. The first time Kirsten and I hit the lake, I wasn't sure this whole thing was going to turn out too well. Zero visibility in the water made determining direction and distance nearly impossible. I realized a few strokes into our swim that my feet could be two feet from the bottom or two hundred. With no lap lane dividers to grab onto, it was just us and a lake full of water. All of the sudden, my breaths grew short, and I was struggling for air. Fear had crept in. I knew other people had done this and lived, so I determined to make my heart slow down and force my breathing to adjust. Translation—I cried out to the Lord. A sense of "I can do this" began to flood my emotions, and my body began to line up. I trusted that the God who gave me strength could also calm my fears. Fear truly is a trust issue. Being near to the God of peace dispels fear. God's Word tells us that "perfect love casts out fear" (1 John 4:18, NKJV). As we invite His presence and allow His love to flow into us, our trust in Him and our awareness of His care for us grows. We must trust that He desires our success, not our failure. Kirsten and I went on to participate in our first triathlon, crossing the finish line together! What fun!

As we begin to rest in His watchful keeping over our lives, faith becomes our dominant response. Our time spent with Him yields clear direction, and when coupled with the confidence that comes from His love for us, we're able to boldly step out in faith. There is a quote by Dr. Lilian B. Yeomans that hangs on my refrigerator. For years, my family has been exposed to these challenging words. "God delights in His children stepping out over the aching void with nothing under their feet but the Word of God." That kind of faith-walking doesn't take place without deliberate faith-building. Immersing ourselves in prayer and reading God's life-giving words are our ticket to that first step of faith. Once the first step is taken, the next ones tend to be successively easier because our confidence has grown that God will indeed catch us if we stumble.

As we step out, God gives us further instruction. Several years ago, God put in my heart a desire to take my first ministerial course. I had no idea that pursuing these courses would dominate my next six years and lead to God's call on my life to preach His gospel. I simply followed His instruction to enter the program and take that first course. At the time, our church only offered one course every three months in the ministerial program, so I had to take whichever course happened to be offered. I laugh now as I look back on the only course available as I entered the program—Sermon Preparation. My very first sermon was preached in front of my seven classmates. I think it lasted about eleven minutes!

In the realm of preparation, we want God to move quickly so we can get to the "good stuff." But, as it turns out, God *is* the "good stuff!" Preparation isn't about skills attained or positioning for what's yet to come. If those things are necessary to what God's got planned, He'll add them in as needed. Preparation is about right hearts and quiet strength gained by being with Him. He is our goal. *He* is our achievement, *He* is our reward. In seasons of preparation, we may often feel like we're not "getting anywhere." But, that's exactly where He wants us—nowhere other than at His feet.

The Bible teaches us not to despise humble positions and small beginnings. Our obedience is the central issue, and relationship with *Him* is the focus. God doesn't require us to seek all the answers before we get started. As a matter of fact, He reserves information to release to us along the way. Trust Him. Follow His lead. He is completely trustworthy. Each step won't always make sense as you move forward, but that's because we can't see the whole plan. Just do what He puts in front of you to do today.

Your reward lies in your relationship to Him and your obedience, not in the finished product. That thinking is contrary to the way our world operates. The world applauds accomplishment, but God rewards faithful steps of obedience. Embracing preparation is simply taking God's ordered steps in our lives and trusting Him with the outcome. When we rush toward the accomplishment, we make wrong turns. If we'll just take one step at a time with our eyes focused on Him, we'll choose rightly.

One of the most beautiful outcomes of embracing preparation is patience. We learn to wait for instruction. We learn to wait for God's best plan. Picture yourself in a maze, running aimlessly toward the prize. After bumping into obstacles and dead ends, we find ourselves frustrated and full of bumps and bruises. We finally stop to reevaluate our position and our options. With deliberate, thoughtful action, we begin again. If, in the pursuit of our dreams, we'll seek *Him*, God will straighten out our path before us. This puts God out ahead of us, rather than us running ahead of His plan. Slow down, and embrace the process of preparation. He knows what He's doing in us, and the end product will be good if we'll trust Him!

Chapter 3

Tending the Heart

"Above all else, guard your heart, for everything you do flows from it." — Proverbs 4:23 (NIV)

WALKING IN LOVE and achieving a dream can be a difficult balance. Since our tendency is to eliminate as much of the time between dream-conception and dream-realization as possible, we easily blow past the joys daily living can bring. One of those joys is walking in love toward the people with which God has chosen to surround us. We must remember that *people* take precedence over *achievement.*

In our busy society, we are a driven people. Time drives us. Schedules drive us. Lack drives us. Self-importance drives us. The need to be needed drives us. We're always moving toward solutions to and elimination of anything that causes us discomfort. Admittedly, we do need to be focused on living excellently, but not at the expense of quiet contentment. Contentment simply places promotion in the hands of God. People often mistake contentment for complacency, which are not equal in definition. Lacking motivation for improvement is complacency. Contentment is desiring to remain in the center of God's will, wherever that may be today.

We are called to be content, and when we are, we tend to live more graciously toward others. We no longer see them as a means to get ahead or another thing to be managed. We see them as the creation they are. People are the image of God Himself wrapped in unique packaging. How dare we use others for our own advancement! Selfishness is fully on display when we live discontented, hurried lives.

Unfortunately, our families suffer most from our state of discontent. We become distracted by our need to fill the void inside us, rather than focusing on those we've been assigned to lead. Parents work long hours to buy more or simply to "feel" appreciated. Perhaps you're known by your colleagues as the "hero." You always know how to save the day. Feels good! But, your kids know you as the absent parent who can't give affirmation out of an empty life. We have a responsibility to our families to settle the contentment issue on the inside of us so we can create an atmosphere of acceptance, peace, and love in them. Peace and rest are companions to contentment. People are desperately drawn to others who seem to have found these treasures.

Learning to live out of a rested, contented life is truly an art. It must be practiced and maintained. It is beautiful, but easily eludes us. Most people never strip down their lives enough to reach contentment. Constant running, buying, talking, texting, traveling, and entertaining drives us away from living a quiet, contented life. Reducing those destructive habits requires ongoing self-discipline. Eventually, if we keep moving faster than we were designed to move, we'll experience the fallout of a worn-out body, neglected or destroyed relationships, and an empty spirit. As we spend time letting God pour into us, *His* perspective becomes *our* perspective, and we will learn to value people over achievement.

The all-out pursuit of a dream can produce the same damaging results as an unbalanced life. The achievement of the dream becomes paramount, ignoring the people God has assigned to us during our journey. Rushing to the end goal of a dream can feel as if we've produced achievement, but if we've not grown other people along the way, the accomplishment is hollow. Growing up in Skyline Wesleyan Church, under the leadership of Dr. John Maxwell, taught me some crucial people skills. The greatest lesson I remember learning is: If I come to the end of my life and the people who were following me didn't surpass me in influence for the Kingdom of God, I didn't do my job. That thought alone has guided many of my decisions in dealing with people. If I have the opportunity to shine, but it's to the neglect of those around me, it probably isn't God. Helping others achieve their dreams is the most effective ticket to achieving mine. God isn't interested in our list of accomplishments; He's interested in our hearts for Him and others.

Our ability to love others comes directly from our willingness to let God love us. We mistakenly believe that love is manufactured in our own hearts. We try to love others from our own selfishness and pride. It doesn't work very well! Since the only source of true love is God Himself, we have no other means to gain it except to spend time allowing Him to love us. That's not an easy task for some. It requires us to be still and devote our focus to Him. While the tasks and busyness of achievement call to us unrelentingly, we must set them aside and simply rest in His presence. There, He reminds us that our identity is in Him, not in what we accomplish. We are loved for who we are, not what we do. It's that same perspective we must have for the people around us. Getting to know them (truly getting to know them) must become a priority. What brings them pleasure? Who are the most important people in their lives? What direction is God taking with their future? We must take the time to draw their dreams out and participate in their journey. It seems counterintuitive to help someone else with their dreams when we want to be achieving our own. But, somehow, God advances our journey as we assist others in theirs. That's just how He works.

During the past three years, I spent several months volunteering in four areas in the community—a refugee center, our city's juvenile detention center, area hospitals, and a program for feeding the homeless people of Nashville. Although I'd love to say I did it out of the goodness of my heart, my motivation was a little less humanly noble—obedience. God appointed me to spend a little time simply giving to others. My own circumstances seemed to have a chokehold on my dreams, and my desperation was rising. Rather than continuing to focus on my own stall-out, God shifted my attention onto others.

The refugees I encountered at the center had come from all over the world, brought to the United States by our government for relocation. Most of them came out of refugee camps in third-world nations. Some spoke very little English, and the need for a patient, friendly face was enormous. I could give that! Others were further along and ready to study for the U.S. Citizenship test. Being a former English teacher, I could help with that as well. Honestly, there was outwardly nothing in it for me, except the joy of helping someone in need. That was exactly where God wanted me, focused on others, not myself. Of course, in the end, I was the one transformed by the experience. God showed me how to love those I would have formerly considered completely outside my sphere of influence. He simply used the experience to shift my perspective away from my own need.

The time spent ministering in the juvenile detention center yielded the same results, but with a bit of a twist. Two Christian men joined me as we met with these young people for an hour each week to share the gospel. Because it's a detention center, the population constantly rotated, giving us a different audience each week. My first meeting with these male, teenage detainees was anything but encouraging. After teaching in a Christian school environment for years, imagine my surprise when these young inmates showed disrespect toward my position of authority! My Bible lesson had been prepared, and I expected that they would listen with sincere interest. Their subdued catcalls and interruptions reminded me that *I* was the intruder in their inhospitable environment. About halfway through my lesson, I closed my Bible and informed these disrespectful young men that I had no intention of finishing if they had no intention of listening! My naive approach reeked of prideful arrogance. I left that night a little mad and more than a little humiliated.

God is so graciously patient with me. He gently reminded me that He had fully equipped me to minister to these young men, but I would need to adjust my approach. Instead of coming *at* them with information, the Holy Spirit instructed me to tell them the stories of the Bible in a friendly manner, guiding each story toward the sacrifice of His Son on the cross. Week after week, I would simply abandon my notes and, in story fashion, recount the extraordinary lives of Daniel, David, Samson, Elijah, and others. As I neared the "altar call," the Holy Spirit had their rapt attention. Those young men realized their need for Christ and prayed the prayer of salvation. I stood amazed week after week at God's faithfulness. Through the preparation of prayer and God's boundless love, salvation was the most natural conclusion at the end of each meeting for these young men. And God did something wonderful for me in the process—He allowed me to practice giving an altar call week after week after week. I would have never assumed God would use a juvenile detention center to develop my ability to guide messages to a moment of salvation. Step by step obedience—there's nothing like it! Keep an open heart toward the people God puts in your path. He'll use them to develop a heart of love in you and move you one step closer to your dream.

As I mentioned, I also spent a significant amount of time in area hospitals. The words "hospital visitation" can send some well-meaning folks into the fetal position. Many people avoid hospitals like the plague (no pun intended). I don't know what it is about me (I've always been a little different), but I love ministering in hospitals. Over the last seven months, one lady in particular stands out, and I will forever remember my experience with her. She had leukemia, and I was her Sunday school teacher at church. Weekly, whether I was visiting other hospitalized patients or not, I would make the trip downtown to visit with her. She had such a devoted heart for God. It seemed she and I found in each other a connection—we both loved pursuing the presence of God. Over those months in the hospital, we prayed, talked about the Lord, walked through shortened versions of the Sunday school lessons I had taught in her absence, and worshipped together in song. Nurses would come in and linger just to listen to the conversation. The family of this beautiful lady became near to my heart. She was such an amazing influence on everyone around her.

One day when all of her family had gathered in her room, I felt an urgency to pray over her. What I thought was a prayer meant just for her turned out to be so much more. The family members left the room to give us a few minutes to talk and pray, except for her brother. I asked if he'd like to pray with us, and he said that he would. As I rounded the corner to "Amen," I asked him where he was with God. He said he wasn't saved, but wanted to be. Right then, right there, in heart-felt prayer, he yielded himself to God's dominion in his life. The ultimate healing prayer is the prayer of salvation.

My heart hurts just a little now as I write this. Two days ago, we held her funeral. As I greeted each family member, I recalled the tears, the prayers, the songs, the pain, and the victories over the last seven months. The family graciously asked me to speak at the funeral. I was honored to publicly share some of those precious memories.

I'm amazed at God's goodness. Within the context of loving people in His name, God gave me the opportunity to learn what it is to minister to sick and hurting people, to comfort those around them, and to always be mindful of leading people into the presence of Christ. No ministerial book or class could ever teach as well.

I am truly humbled by the way God has placed opportunities in front of me. On my own, I don't know that I would have willingly participated in feeding the homeless people of Nashville under the Jefferson Street Bridge every Tuesday night. Wasn't this typical of the dangerous areas Mom always warned me about growing up? Since it was my daughter, Kirsten, who started ministering there first, I didn't have any excuses! My second lovely daughter, Heather, quickly followed Kirsten's example. My husband worked late most evenings each week, and my son had worship team practice, which left me literally sitting at home by myself on Tuesday nights. With a swift kick from the Holy Spirit, I joined my daughters in ministering to some very needy folks. And, I have never been happier to serve! People from churches all over Nashville come together to serve under the bridge on Tuesday nights, where dinner is provided, the gospel is preached, God's name is lifted high in worship, and our guests leave loaded down with groceries and clothing/hygiene items. Why would I want to be anywhere else on a Tuesday night?

There is an incredible satisfaction in sharing a Christ-filled smile and making new friends among people I would never normally come in contact with.

God just keeps breaking down barriers in me! He's teaching me to love those I probably would have previously judged. Through my own family's financial struggles over the last few years, God reminded me that I haven't been so far removed from circumstances that landed some of these precious folks in their current situations. Just being human makes us vulnerable, and God is the only One who gets credit for keeping our heads above water! Let Him create in you a heart that is tender and sensitive to the needs of the people around you. The less we make our lives about us, the more content we'll live.

Chapter 4

Keeping an Open Hand

"Your heavenly Father already knows all your needs, and he will give you all you need from day to day if you live for him and make the Kingdom of God your primary concern." — Matthew 6:32b-33 (NLT)

URING MY JOURNEY of preparation, I've stumbled upon a principle that no one pursuing their dream seems to be exempt from learning. This principle is what I refer to as keeping an open hand. It's our human nature to hold on to what we have with a closed fist. Our selfish behavior as children reveals our true nature, and to be honest, without God pressing us to change, we continue our selfishness throughout adulthood. Keeping a tight grasp on our possessions, titles, relationships, and dreams allows us to falsely believe we control our lives. When we hold these things too tightly, God has no choice but to loosen our grip.

The real issue is trust. Do we trust God's ways and His leading enough to open our hands and let Him remove or add what will mold us into His image and move us toward His purpose? It's easy to say yes, but when God gets serious about teaching us this principle, it's anything but easy! Posing a few questions will help you put the difficulty in perspective. When you're walking in obedience and your bank account is uncomfortably close to zero, will you stay the course and trust Him? When you lose your position as CEO and find a job as head janitor, will you bend your knee in humble gratitude for His provision? When you've poured your heart into your children for eighteen years and they move into their college dorm rooms, will you thank God for the time you've had with them and release them to discover their own destinies with God? When your dream hits a brick wall (and all God-given dreams do), will you trust the Giver of Life to revive it in His timing?

There is no easy way around learning this principle of keeping an open hand. It must be painfully mastered to walk in your destiny. In Matthew 6:32-33 (NLT), Jesus teaches that,

> "...Your heavenly Father already *knows all your needs,* and He will give you all you need from *day to day* if you live for Him and make the *Kingdom of God your primary concern*" (italics mine).

I want to emphasize three aspects of this verse as we examine keeping an open hand.

The first part of Matthew 6:32-33 says that God knows what we need (even before we do). We tend to approach God as if our circumstances have taken even

Him by surprise. He already knows your electric bill will skyrocket, you'll owe more on your taxes than you anticipated, your teenager will need dental work, and your son's feet will grow two sizes overnight! Learning not to panic when the "unexpected" comes your direction is step one.

I have developed my own method of dealing with these panic-producers. When I encounter a bill I cannot fit in the budget, necessary clothes replacement for my six foot, two inches (and growing) seventeen-year-old son, a broken appliance that I don't have the money to replace, or college tuition that's breathing down my neck, I simply list my needs on a piece of paper headed with the Scripture from Matthew 6:32-33. I leave it on the counter and walk away. Inevitably, God somehow meets every single need. I check them off one by one as provision comes, and soon, I'm prepared to start a new list.

The true test of trust is in leaving that list on the counter, not mentally carrying it around. In the very next verse in Matthew 6, Jesus admonishes us not to worry about tomorrow. He knows what's coming our direction, and He already has a solution. As we use wisdom to steward well what He has given us, we must trust that He will take care of the rest.

The second part of Matthew 6:32-33 I want to emphasize says that God will give us what we need from *day to day*. I find it much easier to trust Him when my bank account is full. (I hope you sensed my sarcasm!) However, we don't truly learn trust and keeping an open hand until we find ourselves out of resources. So, don't be surprised when you walk through financially lean weeks, months, and perhaps years. As I said earlier, there's just no easy way to master this trust issue.

God sort of conned me into learning day to day reliance. My husband and I had walked through financially tight times before, so it would take close to a zero balance in our checking and savings before I'd consider hitting the panic button. Would you like to guess the balance? About eight months prior to this situation, God had specifically instructed me to pray that He would sustain us while I waited for Him to open the door to my next step in the dream process. This was particularly difficult because two months prior to *those* words, He had instructed me to resign my teaching position. So, not only did I *not* have a job, but He told me *not* to go find one. Instead, I was to spend time in prayer and study and volunteer my time in our church and in the community. In the meantime, my husband had gone through a job loss of his own and recently found a position at half of his previous salary. The bottom line was that our income settled in at a third of what it had been for several years. With two kids in college and one approaching his senior year in high school... well, you get the point!

There were several times in those long months that we were literally putting gas in the cars and putting food on the table *day by day*. Each time the circumstances grew tight, it got a little easier to just shrug our shoulders and know that God would, once again, come through.

I don't want to neglect to comment on part of the emotional struggle I experienced through these financial lessons. Because I had a very specific word from

God, I had to stay the course and wait for Him to provide. If you're a go-getter like me, that was one of the most difficult exercises God has put me through. I had to fight guilt and self-condemnation for not "rescuing" my family financially. I could have put aside God's instructions and gotten some sort of job to ease the situation. But for me, it would have been direct disobedience. You may ask, "Debbie, how did you know those difficult instructions were truly from God?" Each person must develop their own sensitivity to the Holy Spirit's voice. Hearing Him clearly is critical. However, God always backs His verbal instructions to me with His Word. Soon after He told me to pray that He would sustain us, my eyes fell on the following verses as I was reading through the book of Psalms:

"Surely God is my help; the Lord is the one who sustains me" (Psalm 54:4, NIV)

"Cast your cares on the Lord and He will sustain you; He will never let the righteous be shaken" (Psalm 55:22, NIV).

Also, if God hadn't been in those instructions, our bills would have gone unpaid. There is absolutely no other reasonable explanation for making it through two very lean years with all of our bills paid. As I look back over those difficult years, I am incredibly grateful for *so* much time in His presence, for the serving opportunities at church and in the community, and for the shaping process God has led me through. I promise you that I would not have chosen His method on my own! I'm so glad God drew me into the learning curve one step at a time.

WHAT ABOUT

45

WHitney ?

The third portion of Matthew 6:32-33 that I would like to emphasize is that the day to day provision is ours *as we make the Kingdom of God our primary concern*. Ask yourself what your primary concern is. If you're honest with yourself, you may say job, family, happiness, provision, or your health. God's Kingdom, His church, His will, His calling on your life, and His desires must take precedence. That doesn't sound difficult until you're called to sacrifice in order to put His Kingdom first. Above all else, knowing Him through purposeful pursuit sets our dependency squarely on Him, where it belongs. So, no matter His instructions, or life's circumstances, our trust in Him will keep us steady.

Holding relationships loosely can be even more difficult than keeping an open hand with our finances. Our love and emotional connection with those close to us is God-induced. In our humanness, however, we tend to intertwine the God-given love with emotional dependency. When people leave us by choice or death, it rocks our emotional stability. Grief is a normal human emotion, but the key to healing from grief is to hold our relationships before the Lord with an open hand. *He* is our source for our every emotional need. It's easy to rely on our spouses or children to meet those needs, but they weren't designed to be our source. Parents often become so wrapped up in their children's lives that attempting to function without them close at hand is crippling. Just as a mother bird pushes her babies out of the nest so they'll learn to fly, we also must encourage our children to try out their wings and fly. God's plans for their lives are good, and His Kingdom depends on their engagement.

Although holding our immediate family in care before the Lord ought to be a primary objective, we must see the larger family that God has given us. There is absolutely no substitute for the church, the family of God. There will be times that a family member dies, distances themselves, or deserts us. Although emotional pain results, we'll recover more quickly if we'll keep our eyes firmly fixed on God and our hearts open to the love of the family of God. We need each other. If you've experienced loss in your personal relationships, loosen the grip around your heart. Let others love you. Soon, you'll find yourself able to love freely again. God's healing is complete, if we'll allow it to be. An open, pliable heart invites proper perspective. Perspective helps us shift our focus off of our own pain and the difficulty of our circumstances. When God says to put His Kingdom first, that means shifting our focus off our lives and onto the bigger picture of His Kingdom purposes.

Paul and Silas stand as an example of looking past the obvious impossibilities and praising God directly into a solution of Divine proportion. Paul had just cast a demon out of a fortune-telling girl who had been making her master a lot of money. He was not at all pleased about losing his "investment," and ordered Paul and Silas beaten, arrested, and put in the dungeon prison. Incarcerated, chained, and bleeding, they could have easily nursed a "woe is me" attitude, but instead, they chose to begin singing praise to the only One who could deliver them. God showed up, freed them by shaking things up (an earthquake), and, in the process, proved His power to the others nearby. Here is the official account from Acts 16:25-30 (NLT):

Around midnight, Paul and Silas were praying and singing hymns to God, and the other prisoners were listening. Suddenly, there was a great earthquake, and the prison was shaken to its foundations. All the doors flew open, and the chains of every prisoner fell off! The jailer woke up to see the prison doors wide open. He assumed the prisoners had escaped, so he drew his sword to kill himself. But Paul shouted to him, "Don't do it! We're all here!" Trembling with fear, the jailer called for lights and ran to the dungeon and fell down before Paul and Silas. He brought them out and asked, "Sirs, what must I do to be saved?"

Your key to keeping correct perspective is to be a worshiper. Worship restores joy in the midst of sorrow, hope in the midst of despair, and gratitude in the midst of pain. As God sees us worshipping Him even when the circumstances of our despair don't budge, He is pleased. Faith, then, is in obvious operation in our lives, and faith is what pleases Him. Hebrews 11:6 (NLT) reminds us that "it is impossible to please God without faith." Open your mouth, and let praise flow from your lips, even when you have no idea how God will come through in your current situation. It's not your job to know *how*. It's your job to know that *He will.*

So god... what's wrong? Either something is wrong, or we're expecting too much. so...

48

← what is the truth?

Chapter 5

Gaining Influence

"It is in developing others that we truly succeed." — Harvey Firestone

I WOULD LOVE TO give you a five-step process over how to "win friends and influence people," but the kind of influence I'm speaking of is hewn out of brokenness and humility. *The process,* as we discussed earlier, has a way of digging to the core of our being to find out what really motivates us. Unfortunately, I found pride lurking at the center of most of my dreams and desires. Because He is committed to our growth and maturity, God methodically and carefully exposes those misguided motives to bring our hearts back around to love. All of our actions must always come back to love. Without His love, none of our efforts matter. 1 Corinthians 13:1-3 (NLT) makes this very clear for us:

> If I could speak in any language in heaven or on earth but didn't love others, I would only be making

meaningless noise like a loud gong or a clanging cymbal. If I had the gift of prophecy, and if I knew all the mysteries of the future and knew everything about everything, but I didn't love others, what good would I be? And if I had the gift of faith so that I could speak to a mountain and make it move, without love I would be no good to anybody. If I gave everything I have to the poor and even sacrificed my body, I could boast about it; but if I didn't love others, I would be of no value whatsoever.

As God burns away the wrong and establishes the right, an amazing thing begins to happen. Submission to His way, His purpose, and His desire becomes primary and incredibly influential. When a wild horse is placed into the hands of a skilled horseman, that horse experiences forced submission until it is "broken." Once broken, the horse is useful, being guided by its rider. Our lives are really no different. Placed into the loving hands of our Creator, He presses us until we are broken. As a stallion eventually submits to its rider, there is nothing more beautiful to God than His child submitted to His guiding hand. The peace and humility that are companions to submission produce a beauty evident to people watching our lives. "Self" takes a back seat, and God shines through our brokenness. The struggle, the yielding, the submission, the pain, the brokenness, and the humility make us a magnet for those going through this process of change as well.

So, then, there is benefit to letting people into our process. Admitting to God's pressure and owning up to our resistance makes us humanly attractive in a world where the appearance of perfection has become

incredibly unattractive. Brokenness is generally un-
wanted in our lives. It's usually brought on by devastating circumstances, which leave us nowhere to turn but
to God. A strange thing happens, though, if we'll find
our way into God's presence and be quiet before Him.
As we yield to His leading, He'll gather us into His care
as a mother hen gathers her chicks under her wings.
There, we are quieted. There, we are sheltered. There,
we are nourished, even in the midst of our pain.

Although I have desired and sought the Lord for as
long as I can remember, being sheltered by Him in the
midst of a long and violent storm has, by far, grown my
intimacy with Him in unparalleled measure. I don't
like pain. I don't like devastating circumstances. But,
I have found that when I make Him my refuge, I like
the outcome! We grow in relationship with Him as we
come close, drawing comfort and strength from His
presence. This is why James said,

> Dear brothers and sisters, whenever trouble comes
> your way, let it be an opportunity for joy. For when
> your faith is tested, your endurance has a chance
> to grow. So let it grow, for when your endurance is
> fully developed, you will be strong in character and
> ready for anything. — James 1:2-4 (NLT)

It's hard for us to believe that our greatest growth
comes through our pain, but God knew we wouldn't
willingly subject ourselves to intense growth sessions
without some prodding. Trials become our prodding.
Notice the last line of verse four: "...when your endurance is fully developed, you will be strong in character
and ready for anything." How can we possibly be ready
for anything? We can by hiding ourselves in Him and

letting Him mature us. Verse twelve in this same chapter goes on to say, "God blesses the people who patiently endure testing." The word *patiently* just raised the bar! Lean into Him, and let God have His way in your life. Embrace trials that come your direction knowing they'll make you stronger in Him, and allow Him to reward you with His rich blessings.

What's even greater than our own growth and reward in the process is watching others influenced by our response. Each one of us is surrounded by people we influence. Some, such as our immediate family members, have the closest access to us and are recipients of our greatest influence. And, as we pull others close to us, we give them a bird's eye view into our sometimes messy lives. Still, others are simply curious onlookers, but they all receive, at differing levels, influence from the way we live and the decisions we make along the way.

My three children have been my most accessible audience. As my children grew, I chose to dream in front of them. I wanted them to achieve all that God had planned for their lives, and what better way than to dream God-sized dreams in my own life. My plan stayed on track until my unfulfilled dreams stretched from months to years, climbing past a decade. Talk about disillusionment! At the end of my own efforts, God was supposed to present me with the opportunities I had longed for, prepared for, and believed for. God had other ideas. Learning that God just doesn't work that way was probably more the lesson than all those years of my own preparation. The unknown future that loomed in front of me and the empty disappointment that surrounded me became fertile ground for the most influential marks I would leave on my children's lives.

What happens when we come to the end of ourselves, the end of a hard-earned road that seems to have produced absolutely nothing? We're tempted to give up on the dream, and in bitterness, write off the idea that God comes through in the end. But if we do that, we abandon the process too soon. Coming to the end of ourselves is the very place God does His best work. It's also the most difficult place to be. Holding on to a dream that appears to be dead or unattainable solidifies the inevitability of the transformation going on inside us. Maybe in the emptiness God is holding up a mirror to show us how He is growing us and strengthening us. Without the possibility of the death of our dream, there cannot be true fulfillment.

Ever watchful, my children have celebrated with me, cried with me, waited with me, encouraged me, and will someday soon rejoice with me over the fulfillment of God's plan. I know beyond a shadow of a doubt that God will bring the fulfillment. That may sound like great faith, but honestly, I simply know He won't allow His great name to be diminished in my children's eyes. As they have shifted into adulthood, they eagerly watch to see that God truly rewards those who diligently seek Him. He won't let them (or me) down. This journey has become as much about them as it is about finishing the work He began in me. Be observant about who you are influencing. Embrace the mantle of responsibility to reflect God's nature through your attitudes and actions.

As in everything God does, my children aren't the only recipients of the influence of my journey. What

I didn't realize in the midst of my own struggles was that God was using my painful experiences to influence ripples of people beyond my immediate reach. People I do not know personally continue to comment about the peace that seems to accompany my life. I recently attended a Christmas party for one of our church's Sunday school groups. As I strolled across the room, greeting people along the way, a woman stopped me. Completely catching me off guard, she confided, "There's something about you that creates a sense of security wherever you go. When I see you, I know everything's going to be all right." All I know is... it's not me that produces that kind of peace! It's the presence of the Living God in me as I spend time with Him.

Within a short time, I found myself in a similar situation. Walking into a hospital to visit a church member, I stopped by the information desk to verify a room number. The lady working at the desk asked if I was a minister. I assumed she was asking that question prior to giving me confidential information. I answered yes, ready to produce my official, laminated, denomination-issued ministerial card! To my humbled surprise, she responded, "I could tell by the peace in your voice." I didn't need man's credentials; she could tell I had been in His presence. God is the author of peace, so I know when others sense peace, He's at work!

Confidence is another indicator that your purpose is rising within you. Not prideful confidence, but rather an acceptance of the purpose to which He's called you. When you've come to peace with His purpose for your life, anxiety subsides and confident resolution settles in your spirit. The knowledge that He is sovereign over the direction of your life is incredibly freeing.

The influence gained by walking confidently in your God-given purpose trumps worldly success. Why? Because God changes others while He changes you. This reminds us that although He's using our lives in noble ways, our ultimate influence is reflected in the lives around us. We'd like to believe that somehow it's all about us, but it never is! It's all about Him. So, place all of the praise, all of the adoration, and all of the glory where it belongs—squarely on God.

Chapter 6

Learning to Wait

"I would have lost heart unless I had believed that I would see the goodness of the Lord in the land of the living. Wait on the Lord. Be of good courage and He will strengthen your heart. Wait, I say, on the Lord." — Psalm 27:13-14 (NKJV)

Wait is not a four-letter expletive! However, when you're the one who is waiting, it sure does seem like it. Waiting is one of the most difficult, yet necessary, contributors to transformation. Even if God put us through the paces of trials and opposition, but didn't require us to learn the art of waiting, we would emerge still lost in our own self-absorption. Waiting forces us to depend on Him, deepening our trust.

Learning to wait is a discipline. It goes against our human nature, especially in today's culture. Waiting is turning control over to God's timing and method. We want to remain in control, so we have a tendency to manipulate the circumstances, hoping to produce the outcome we're looking for. Resisting that urge and settling into allowing God to work things out in His timing and His way produces maturity in us.

Why is waiting so difficult for us? The basic reason is that we lack perspective. God sees the end from the beginning, and we don't. Think of it as a puzzle. God knows what the big picture looks like. There are many pieces God is bringing into place, positioning us and others for just the right combination of circumstances and timing. However, our focus is limited, so it's hard for us to see the benefit of learning to wait, the benefit of resting in His timing while He completes His positioning. But, that's exactly what He's calling us to do—to rest in Him while we wait.

Lewis Smedes writes, "Waiting is our destiny as creatures, who cannot by themselves, bring about what they hope for. We wait in the darkness for a flame we cannot light. We wait in fear for a happy ending we cannot write. We wait for a not yet that feels like a not ever. Waiting is the hardest work of hope." Thankfully, we have a God who is faithful and desires to bless us and honor us in due time. Scripture reminds us of this.

"For the Lord is a faithful God. Blessed are those who wait for Him to help them." —Isaiah 30:18 (NLT)

"So, humble yourselves under the mighty power of God, and at the right time He will lift you up in honor." —1 Peter 5:6 (NLT)

Waiting isn't easy, and it's often scary. We find ourselves in precarious situations with impossible circumstances surrounding us, and God is seemingly nowhere to be found. And yet, He tells us to wait for Him to help us. Our natural reaction is fear, and instead of waiting on God and His solution, we jump the gun and start making decisions on our own to solve our problems.

1 Samuel 13 illustrates this very situation. With a formidable opponent (the Philistines) closing in, King Saul of Israel was given a clear directive to wait for Samuel the prophet/priest to arrive so that a sacrifice could be made. According to God's law, sacrifices must be carried out by a priest. King Saul was not a priest. He grew weary waiting for Samuel to arrive. The Philistines were gaining strength, ready to attack, and Saul was scared.

King Saul wanted God's blessing before going into battle, but he did not want the price tag of obedience attached to the blessing. Saul unlawfully conducted the sacrifice himself. Samuel arrived, greatly dismayed.

"How foolish!" Samuel exclaimed. "You have disobeyed the command of the Lord your God. Had you obeyed, the Lord would have established your kingdom over Israel forever. But now your dynasty must end, for the Lord has sought out a man after his own heart. The Lord has already chosen him to be king over his people, for you have not obeyed the Lord's command." — 1 Samuel 13:13-14 (NLT)

In one act of disobedience, King Saul derailed his purpose. Unfortunately, Saul gave excuses rather than repenting for his actions. Are you wondering who the man is spoken of in that Scripture, the "man after God's own heart?" That would be King David, whose lineage would eventually lead to the King of Kings, Jesus Christ. Does that mean King David never sinned? No, the difference between Saul and David was that David had a repentant heart. God isn't impressed by our perfection. He's after a humble and contrite heart.

In the heat of impending battle, Saul's actions bore what was in his heart. Like Saul, our true spiritual character is revealed under pressure. When Saul felt that time was running out, he became impatient with God's timing and acted in disobedience. Don't allow impatience to drive you to disobey God. When you know what God wants (and Saul *did* know), follow His plan regardless of the way things look. God often uses delays to test our obedience and patience.

Waiting has certainly never been one of my strong suits. If something needs to be done, and isn't getting done, I'll step in and make it happen. That's not a bad philosophy for some circumstances, but it crosses over to disobedience if it butts heads with God's plan. I'm not proud to say that, in the past, if God hadn't yet opened a door (and I couldn't get it to budge), I'd find a way in through a window. That's the same spirit Saul was dealing with, and it's ugly. As God brought my glaring pride before me, I made the decision to cooperate with His plan to change me. And the change has been painful—and long! When I thought He would open the door to full-time ministry, He didn't. When I thought He might be leading me to another ministry so I could "get on with it," He wasn't. Twenty-two years ago, He planted me in a church under a pastor who still remains my spiritual leader today. My pastor knows

God's calling on my life, and I'm so grateful he's listening to God's timing, not mine. God has not yet released me into His bigger plan, so I wait, walking in obedience right where I'm at.

I remember having a discussion with a staff pastor (we'll call him Larry) about three years ago regarding entering into full-time ministry. By then, God had already course-corrected me and told me to remain under submission to my pastor's lead over my life. So, when Larry asked what my plans were for the future, I chose my words carefully. "Larry, in the past, I have kicked doors open to get what I wanted, but I can't do that anymore. I will wait until God opens the door." His reply was simple, but incredibly telling, "You're a better person than I am." Within one year, he attempted to push his way into the pulpit, and instead, was shown the door. I have prayed for him since the day he left, that there would be reconciliation with our pastor. Without it, Larry's success will be hindered. Those are hard words, but aligning ourselves with the spiritual authority God sets over us builds a solid foundation for the successful fulfillment of God's call.

However heartfelt and noble my words were during my conversation with Larry, *my* wait didn't end anytime soon. God still had much work to do in me. Learning to slow down, to rest, to love, and to better know Him were all still yet to be attained. Be willing to wait for God's timing. You'll find yourself in a ditch somewhere along the way if you don't.

Over the last five years, God has detached from my life those things that I had allowed to define me. My career as an educator went by the wayside when I resigned.

The ministry titles accumulated over the years disappeared when I was side-lined. Any sense of pride I felt as my husband's wife was overshadowed by pain for a period of time as he dealt with his circumstances. God remained my only hope and my place of refuge. Empty and laid bare, I prostrated myself before the Lord, letting Him redefine me as His child and His delight. As I fed on His Word and presence, I gained strength—*His* strength. My heart became free, and my shame melted away. Joy and love filled me to overflowing, allowing me to walk in confident assurance of His constant presence and peace.

Even if we acknowledge the benefits of waiting on God, it isn't easy. However, God offers us a solution—become a person of prayer! Prayer becomes your best defense against fear and rash action. Prayer is simply leaning in close enough to the heart of God that the circumstances don't sway you away from trusting Him and His timing. We often view prayer as trying to get something from God, almost as if we're manipulating Him. Prayer is more about offering our hearts to Him, allowing Him to reshape our desires and priorities. Usually, changing *us* is what fixes situations, not changing the circumstances. God often chooses to carry us *through* trials, morphing us along the way, rather than extracting us from our pain. Remind yourself that He desires good for you even if the learning curve is really steep. Don't shy away from getting honest with God. Open your heart before Him, and let Him have full access to whatever changes He deems necessary. Ask God to show you any areas in which you're acting on your own initiative, and bring them under His authority. Blessing awaits you as you walk in obedience and embrace His timing.

Chapter 7

Refusing to Quit

"I press on toward the goal to win the prize for which God has called me heavenward in Christ Jesus." — Philippians 3:14 (NIV)

WHEN THE WAITING grows long, the temptation to quit can become overpowering. There are more "exit" doors along the last mile of your dream than in all the miles before it. The weariness that can set in makes those doors look incredibly enticing. It's critical at this point to shift your focus onto something other than the wait.

I started running almost five years ago. At that time, a potentially fatal assault attacked my dream, and I desperately needed an outlet. I put on a pair of tennis shoes, walked out my front door, and just ran until I couldn't make my body take one more step. I began to use running for a two-fold purpose—releasing stress and building endurance, spiritually as well as physically.

Out of my need to regain a sense of control over some aspect of my life, I set a goal of running six miles. When I began, I couldn't even run one continuous mile. Even as a competitive gymnast growing up, my strength was not endurance. Appearing physically fit doesn't always equal heart-healthy endurance! Winding through my neighborhood, I would only allow myself to run as far as I could manage without walking. Each day, I would lengthen my distance one or two mailboxes at a time. Within about three months, I had achieved six miles and successfully finished a local 10k race. Self-satisfaction was only momentary; the fight for the deliverance of my dream was about to be a long one, so I set my sights on a half-marathon. Two things stand out in my memory about that first half-marathon. My oldest daughter, Kirsten, chose to drive eight hours home from college to run that race with me. That's commitment! Also, the race ended inside Nashville's LP Field, and each runner's name was announced as they passed over the electronic sensor. Our accomplishment was rewarded as we crossed the finish line!

Still awaiting the fulfillment of my dream, I've run five half-marathons, and am preparing for my second Olympic-length triathlon. If God waits too much longer, I may have to sign-up for an Iron Man race!

Perspective plays a huge part in the ability to endure the desert experiences on the road to dream fulfillment. Being able to keep the end goal in mind during the difficulties is the difference between living above your circumstances and drowning in them. During my four especially difficult years of waiting, I experienced seasons of accusation, isolation, and loneliness. Those seasons are not uncommon to dream chasers, but that knowledge doesn't make the experiences any less painful.

One technique I used to cope with the emotional toll was focusing on a visual image God gave me. I imagined I was standing on the beach in the middle of a hurricane with incredibly forceful winds blowing against me. The wind fought to throw me off balance, the sand pelted my face, and the threat of sheer power stood ready to overtake me. But, as I pictured myself in this scenario, I knew that God's power was stronger and able to keep my feet planted, unmovable. Though the hurricane was horrific, I knew I'd be able to outlast it.

Your calling (purpose, assignment, destiny) must be preeminent in your thinking as you walk through the onslaught of difficulty. Remember also that our battle is not against people. It's against Satan, who is our real enemy. So, when the people you've loved and trusted throw accusations your direction or turn their backs on you, don't hold it against them. Pray that God would go before you and repair the relationships. In my experience, those people who brought accusations against me came back around, and God honored me for keeping a right attitude toward them. He'll do the same for you!

My daily prayer time always includes three things: favor with those in authority over me, joy overflowing, and far-reaching influence. Keeping right relationships is critical. That's why I pray for favor. We're all human, and we sometimes say and do things that rub against people's comfort zones. Asking God to smooth out our interactions can mean the difference between pleasant relationships and friction. Learning to be a people-person is beneficial!

I mentioned that I also pray for joy. Joy is like the oil that makes an engine run frictionless. A warm smile has a way of diffusing potentially unpleasant interactions. People are drawn to those with a joyful spirit and a positive outlook on life. Louis Satchel Page, a black baseball pitcher during the prejudiced times of segregation, said, "Work like you don't need the money; dance like no one's watching; and love like you've never been hurt." God's joy inside of us has the ability to push past the responses of the people around us and lead them to a greater future.

Your life was meant to spill over on to others. We refer to it as influence. Influence can be negative or positive, and it's up to us to choose how we saturate the people around us. The analogy of the thermometer versus the thermostat demonstrates this point. If we adopt the thermometer mindset, we simply reflect the temperature of the people around us. They have partial control over our emotional state. If we employ the thermostat mindset, *we* set the temperature for the people around us.

With influence comes responsibility and maturity. Part of not giving up on the pursuit of your dream is the steadiness of maturity. People need to see that you hold steady during times of difficulty. They are able to find comfort in knowing that your circumstances don't knock you off your feet. It gives them hope that they also will withstand life's hurricanes. Embrace the influence God gives you while you're gaining strength through your own battles of endurance.

God *will* finish the work He started in you. It's easy to feel lost in the midst of the process because we can't see the finish line. God knows exactly where that line is, and He's moving you steadily in the right direction. We must trust that He knows how much adversity we can handle, and that He won't allow us to be crushed under the weight of the trials. Keep your eyes trained on Him, and He will safely deliver you to your destination. Ultimately, this is *His* calling, *His* purpose engraved upon our lives, and *He* desires to complete it even more than we do. Just resolve to never give up. Trust Him.

...these things I plan won't happen right away. Slowly, steadily, surely, the time approaches when the vision will be fulfilled. If it seems slow, wait patiently, for it will surely take place. It will not be delayed. — Habakkuk 2:3 (NLT)

CPSIA information can be obtained
at www.ICGtesting.com
Printed in the USA
FSOW02n2354041016
25657FS

9 781943 294138